When it's time to call the FUNERAL DIRECTOR

Keeping you connected to your loved one throughout their funeral process, and showing how you can be involved

Garth Wright

First Edition

A catalogue record for this book is available from
The National Library of New Zealand
ISBN: 1453829717
ISBN-13: 9781453829714

CONTENTS

INTRODUCTION

Garth Wright was born in a gold mine hospital in Carletonville, South Africa in 1969. On completing his schooling he studied a Bachelor of Arts in Theology, while working with youth in the community. He found exercise and outdoor activity to be a very effective tool in connecting people of all ages to themselves, and building self esteem. He obtained a Diploma in exercise and fitness instruction and worked as a personal trainer, approaching health and fitness from a holistic point of view. His approach empowered his clients to be able to manage their own health and well-being once they felt they had reached a point where they no longer needed close supervision.

He then changed direction by studying to become a close protection officer. He worked for the African Bodyguard and Security Services Association, where he was responsible for the safety of foreign business people and their families for the duration of their stay in the country. One of his main functions was to educate and enable each member of the family to be an active part of their own safety.

He now lives in New Zealand with his wife and three children, where he works as a funeral director in Auckland. When asked why he has chosen yet another new direction in his new country, he said "it is not a new direction at all; it feels as if I am coming home!"

Whatever field Garth works in, he has the ability to throw light on an area, and enable the individual to take control.

PREFACE

As human beings, we are one of the creatures on this earth who mourn the loss of our own. I meet people so obviously shocked when someone they love has died. This sometimes shows in the person being mentally unclear, emotionally numb, and quite vulnerable at our meeting. This may make them very open to suggestion regarding the funeral process of their loved one, and possibly unable to make clear, assertive decisions.

"What do people normally do?" is a common question that I am asked. By this question I understand the need to channel the funeral process in a way that is culturally and socially seen as appropriate and "normal".

Not so long ago, when we humans lived in small village type communities in many parts of the world, if someone in a family died, it used to be normal for family members to be very involved. A special room in the house would be used for the person to be laid out in. They would stay in this room, at home, surrounded by family and visited by friends in the days before their funeral service. The 'elders' in the family would make all of the funeral arrangements, and coordinate the actual funeral day with the local clergy or spiritual leader.

Nowadays, we have a more modern funeral home. There is the obvious convenience for the modern family in this *'out of the private home and into the funeral home'* arrangement, but there is also a loss to the family. It is too easy to allow the modern funeral home, with all of its 'professional services', to override a family's personal need to stay connected to their loved one, and to be involved in their funeral process, if they wish to be.

As to what is normal, ask rather "what feels right for you?" We are not emotional clones. We are each unique. We perceive life through our own eyes, with our own beliefs and values. The way we experience the loss of someone dear to us is very personal, and needs to be recognized and accommodated for. I believe that personalised grieving is essential at this time.

It is in this area particularly that I feel the people affected most by someone's death are often unaware of the ways that they can stay involved with and be connected to their loved one right up to the day of their funeral.

Some funeral directors prefer to keep the funeral process as simple as possible for the family. It is often the case that unless the family know about certain options that are available and specifically ask for them, they may not take place. The days before the funeral itself may be full of missed opportunities that could have helped close family and friends to personalize their grief, and to pay tribute in an appropriate and meaningful way.

Don't allow yourself to be kept out of the funeral process of someone you love because of the specialized nature and disjointedness of our modern societies. Just because a funeral home has taken your loved one into their care, does not mean that you cannot be actively involved with them in the days leading up to their funeral.

This book is written to show you how you can work with your funeral home, with your funeral director, to bring back some close and personal elements to the funeral of someone you love, that used to be 'normal' in days gone by. My hope is that these pages will share information with you that will make you feel prepared, and give you a sense of focus and personal power in the midst of your sadness, your loss.

I am writing from the perspective of an urban New Zealand funeral director. Some laws and procedures will be different if you live in another part of the world, but I hope that there will still be some things that will help you, that you can grab hold of and use no matter where you are. We are all human after all.

SO WHAT DOES A FUNERAL DIRECTOR ACTUALLY DO?

They:

- take care of the transportation of a person who has died
- provide specialised care for the body
- meet with the family and friends of the person who has died, to plan the 'pre funeral' and 'funeral day' details, and act as an event coordinator
- make all of the planned details a reality
- serve the family on the day of the funeral

- facilitate the cremation or burial of the person

- take care of all paperwork.

Within these processes, a funeral director's involvement can be very helpful to you, but there are still many opportunities where you can be very actively involved. As you read, make notes in the side, underline keywords and ear-mark pages. I have left space for more detailed notes should you need it.

If you read this book from cover to cover, you will find some parts to be similar. Please forgive the repetition. I have written this for a person in need to be able to go directly to the chapters that are relevant to them, without having to look up too many references.

PART ONE

CHOOSING A FUNERAL HOME

- It is okay to shop around

- You can use the internet, the yellow pages and word of mouth recommendations.

- Feel free to visit a funeral home

- Have a look around the facilities and get a feel for the place. Meet some of the staff, and see if they are warm and friendly.

- Is the funeral home flexible?

- How accommodating are they to your wishes?

- It is okay to ask for prices

- It is essential that you are happy with and confident in the funeral home which you are about to trust with caring for your loved one.

DOES THERE HAVE TO BE A FUNERAL?

- Fundamental to planning the funeral of someone you love, is how you would like to honour them.

- You do not have to have a service at all. An informal gathering at a meaningful venue may be what you feel would be right.

or

When It's Time to Call the Funeral Director

- You may want your loved one to be privately cremated or buried, and have a memorial service for them at a later date.

or

- You may want a traditional funeral service at a venue of your choosing.

CHAPTER 1

WHEN SOMEONE DIES AT A HOSPITAL OR REST HOME

Let us begin at the point of realisation, when you are first aware that your loved one has died. Following are different scenarios as to where your loved one is when they die, and whether or not you have already chosen a funeral home to help you with them.

WHEN SOMEONE DIES AT A HOSPITAL AND YOU HAVE A FUNERAL HOME

When someone dies at a hospital, make contact with your funeral home. One of the questions you can expect to be asked by your funeral director is whether you would like your loved one to be buried or cremated. Your funeral director wants to start the right process for the person who has died, to ensure that all of their paperwork and legal documentation will be ready. This process can be fast-tracked should your culture or religion require a cremation or burial to take place within a very short time after someone has died. Your funeral director will be in touch with the hospital and ask to be notified the moment the paperwork is ready.

SAYING GOODBYE TO YOUR LOVED ONE AT A HOSPITAL

If you are able to be at your loved one's bedside at the time of their death, the hospital staff are usually able to be very accommodating in allowing you time to grieve and say goodbye in private. Feel comfortable to ask for this time, even though you may have been there for a while already.

If you are elsewhere when the hospital contacts you to inform you of your loved one's death and you would like to see them right away, let the hospital staff know. They will give you the time you need to say goodbye. Some hospitals have rooms that are more private than the ward your loved one has been in, where they can be taken. When you have spent some time with them, and you feel ready for the next step, there are different options as to what happens to their body at this time:

WHAT YOU CAN CHOOSE TO DO

You can tell the nursing staff that they may take your loved one to the hospital mortuary to await collection by your chosen funeral home.

OR

You can contact your funeral home and ask them to fetch your loved one from their ward.

This is a possibility if you are not comfortable with your loved one being taken to the hospital mortuary.

This is what you need to do:

Inform the hospital staff of your decision.

They will then know to contact your funeral home the moment all the necessary paperwork is complete. Once the hospital staff has contacted them, a funeral director will arrive at the hospital. This process may take a few hours.

WHAT YOU CAN CHOOSE TO DO

You can choose not to wait.

You can go home, knowing that your loved one is due to be collected from their ward and taken directly to your funeral home mortuary. Your funeral director will be in contact with you to answer any questions and to arrange a time to meet.

OR

You can wait with your loved one for the funeral directors arrival.

If you choose to wait, the nursing staff will introduce you to the director when they arrive. Your funeral director will ask for your permission to see the person who has died, to see what will need to be done for a safe and dignified transfer from their bed onto the stretcher.

WHAT YOU CAN CHOOSE TO DO

Wait outside of the room as the funeral director moves your loved one onto the stretcher.

OR

You can stay in the room to watch this process.

OR

You can help.

Let the funeral director know that you would like to be involved.

If you choose to stay in the room or to help, this is what generally happens:

- Tell your funeral director that you are ready for them to take your loved one.

- They will bring the stretcher into the room and place it next to the bed. The bed height may be mechanically adjusted to align it with the stretcher. If you want to hug, touch hands or kiss your loved one before they are moved, now is a good time to do so.

- They will be moved onto the stretcher and then safely secured with material belts much like the seat belts from a car. Then they will be covered with a stretcher cover.

- Your funeral director will transfer your loved one to their vehicle. You are welcome to walk with them. Let them know if this is what you would like to do. From here they will go directly to the funeral home mortuary.

WHEN SOMEONE HAS DIED AT A HOSPITAL, AND YOU DO NOT HAVE A FUNERAL HOME

Once you have spent some time with your loved one, you may not be in the right headspace to make funeral home decisions and to deal with all that that entails. This is especially common if you or your loved one have made no special arrangements regarding their funeral wishes. Do not be pressured by the situation. You will work it out one step at a time. You have said goodbye at their bedside, next is to give yourself some time to digest what has happened and to gather your thoughts.

WHAT YOU NEED TO DO

When you are ready, tell the nursing staff that they have your permission to take your loved one to the hospital mortuary until you have decided on which funeral home to use to help with their funeral. Hospital staff will then transfer your loved one to the mortuary.

WHAT YOU CAN CHOOSE TO DO

You can go home, knowing that your loved one is being transferred to the hospital mortuary.

OR

You can stay at the hospital while this transfer is being done.

If you have decided to stay:

WHAT YOU CAN CHOOSE TO DO

You can wait outside of the room as the hospital staff move your loved one onto the stretcher.

OR

You can stay in the room to watch this process.

OR

You can help.

Let the hospital staff know that you would like to be involved in the moving of your loved one onto the stretcher.

WHEN SOMEONE DIES AT A REST HOME AND YOU HAVE A FUNERAL HOME

When someone dies at a rest home, make contact with your funeral home. One of the questions you can expect to be asked by your funeral director is whether you would like your loved one to be buried or cremated. Your funeral director wants to start the right process for the person who has died, to ensure that all of their paperwork and legal documentation will be ready. Your funeral director will be in touch with the rest home and ask to be notified the moment the paperwork is ready. This process can be fast-tracked should your culture or religion require a burial or cremation to take place within a very short time after someone has died.

WHEN SOMEONE DIES AT A REST HOME AND YOU DO NOT HAVE A FUNERAL HOME

When someone moves in to a rest home, one of the requirements is often that there be a nominated funeral home that will be responsible for caring for your loved one should they die whilst in their care. There can be situations though, where for whatever reason, a funeral home may not have been chosen yet.

WHAT YOU NEED TO DO

Choose a funeral home to care for your loved one as soon as you can.
Most rest homes do not have a mortuary facility, and it is important that your loved one's body continues to be cared for in the best possible way.

SAYING GOODBYE TO YOUR LOVED ONE AT A REST HOME

If you are able to be at your loved one's bedside at the time of their death, the rest home staff are usually able to be very accommodating in allowing you time to grieve and say goodbye in private.
If you are elsewhere when the rest home contacts you to inform you of your loved one's death, and you would like to see them right away, let the rest home staff know so that they can inform your funeral home of your wish to spend time with them before they are transferred to the funeral home.
When you are ready for your loved one to be taken to the funeral home, let the rest home staff know. When all of the paperwork is ready, they will notify your funeral director, who will arrive shortly. This whole process may take a few hours.

WHAT YOU CAN CHOOSE TO DO

You can choose not to wait.

When you feel ready, you can go home, knowing that your loved one is due to be collected and taken directly to your funeral home. Your funeral director will be in contact with you to answer any questions and to arrange a time to meet.

OR

You can wait with your loved one for the funeral director's arrival.

If you choose to wait, the rest home staff will introduce you to the director when they arrive. They will ask for your permission to see the person who has died, to see what will need to be done for a safe and dignified transfer from their bed onto the stretcher.

WHAT YOU CAN CHOOSE TO DO

You can wait outside of the room as they shift your loved one onto the stretcher.

OR

You can stay in the room to watch this process.

OR

You can help.

Let the funeral director know that you would like to be involved in the moving of your loved one onto the stretcher.

It is important that you feel comfortable with whatever decision you make.

NOTES

CHAPTER 2

WHEN SOMEONE DIES AT HOME UNDER A DOCTOR'S CARE

People who are unwell and know that they are dying often want to be in the familiar surroundings of their home, with the people they love and who love them around them.

If someone dies at home under a family doctor's treatment and care, the first thing to do is to phone that family doctor.

If you have a chosen funeral home, now is the time to make contact with them as well. The doctor will arrive to confirm that your loved one has died.

When a doctor has been involved with your loved one, there is no urgent need to have them moved right away.

WHAT YOU CAN CHOOSE TO DO

As soon as the doctor has been and left all of the necessary paperwork, you can have your funeral director come and transfer your loved one to their funeral home.

OR

You can keep your loved one at home for a while, allowing family and friends some private time to be with them. It is important not to rush. This can be a very special and peaceful time.

When It's Time to Call the Funeral Director

If this is what you have chosen to do, inform your funeral home of your decision, and discuss a time when they can come.

Here are some guidelines for caring for your loved one at home after they have died:

- Keep them cool. If the person has been lying on an electric blanket, this needs to be turned off now. If they have been covered by many blankets, remove all but one. If it is winter, do not put a heater on in the room. Allow the room temperature to cool their body. Keep them in the shade. Draw the curtains in summer or winter to protect them from direct sunlight. The bacteria that break the body down thrive in warm temperatures.

- If left alone, place a sheet or net over their face.

- Rigor mortis may start to set in. This is the stiffening of the joints that starts about three hours after someone has died, and lasts up to twelve hours, before slowly loosening. There is no need to be concerned. It is a completely natural process that happens in varying degrees to everyone who dies.

There are some conditions that may develop, when it may be best if they are transferred to the funeral home as soon as possible. Once there, they can be kept in a cool room, or they can be embalmed.

These conditions are:

- If their body has any areas of blistering or breaks in the skin.

- If their body has a strong smell of decomposition.

- If areas of their body change colour.

- If there is any swelling on their body, especially of the abdomen.

The information in this block is graphic, and it is not essential that you read it. If you are interested in more detail, you may find it informative.

If their body is leaking any fluids, foam, partial solids or gases from the mouth, nose or rectum, this may indicate gas or fluid build-up inside of their abdominal cavity. This causes internal pressure, which forces discharges out of the body through the path of least resistance.

Any of these conditions may result in a body rapidly breaking down. Contact your funeral director and discuss any concerns with them.

If they feel that there is cause for concern, they will soon arrive, and will ask for your permission to see the person who has died. They will be seeing what will be needed for the safe and dignified transfer of your loved one onto their stretcher. They will ask you when you are ready for them to begin.

WHAT YOU CAN CHOOSE TO DO

You can stay outside of the room while your loved one is moved onto the stretcher.

OR

You can stay in the room to watch the process.

OR

You can help.

If you choose to stay in the room or to help, I will describe what generally happens when someone who has died is fetched from their home, so that you know what to expect:

- Tell your funeral director that you are ready for them to move your loved one.

When It's Time to Call the Funeral Director

- They will bring the stretcher into the room and place it next to the bed. If you want to hug, touch hands or kiss your loved one before they are moved onto the stretcher, now is a good time to do so.

- They will be moved onto the stretcher and then safely secured with material belts much like the seat belts from a car. Finally they will be covered with a stretcher cover.

- A two-man stretcher may be used.This is not on wheels, but is carried. It is easier to manoeuvre around tight corners or up and down stairs.

- Your loved one will be transferred to their vehicle. You are welcome to assist in carrying the stretcher, or to walk alongside. Let your funeral director know if this is what you would like to do.

- From here they will be taken directly to the funeral home mortuary.

You may want your loved one to remain in the care of the funeral home from this time on, or you may want them to be brought back home after their body has been cared for.
Some families have followed me to the mortuary, where they have remained in a private waiting area until their loved one's body has been embalmed. Then they help with their dressing, and assist in placing them into their casket, before having them brought back home. This may take some hours, but the person who has died is surrounded by those who love them from the time of their death right up to them being home again. There they remain until the day of their funeral. *This may not always be possible as certain conditions may need days to care for.*

NOTES

CHAPTER 3

WHEN SOMEONE DIES UNEXPECTEDLY

My hope is that the following information will enable the reader to help someone who has unexpectedly lost their loved one.

If your loved one has died unexpectedly, suspiciously, as the result of an accident, a suicide or suspected criminal action, the police will need to be contacted, as well as your family doctor, if you have one. The coroner and the police will assist and support you, communicating with you throughout this time.

WHAT YOU CAN EXPECT TO HAPPEN WHEN THE POLICE ARRIVE

The police will arrive at the scene, and they will want to be taken to where the person who has died is. They will interview the people or the person who discovered the body and any other people that may help them to get an idea of what happened. They will explain everything that needs to be done, and are professional and discreet. In the case of an unexpected death, they want to find out exactly what caused your loved one to die. When the police are satisfied that they have gathered all the information that they need to start their investigation, they will contact their on-call funeral director. They will be from a funeral home in the area that is responsible for transporting people that have died to the police mortuary, and are simply working for the police in this context. You are under no obligation to use them as your funeral home. They will transfer the person onto the stretcher safely and in a dignified manner.

WHAT YOU CAN CHOOSE TO DO

You can wait away from the area.

OR

You can stay in the area to watch this process.

OR

You can help.

If there is no suspected crime having been committed, it is not uncommon for the police to let you assist. Ask if you may help if this is what you want to do. This may be in the form of moving furniture to make a room more accessible for the stretcher or being involved in the moving of your loved one onto the stretcher.

It is important that you feel comfortable with whatever decision you make. The funeral director will then transfer your loved one to their vehicle. You may assist in carrying the stretcher, or walk with them if you would like to. Your loved one will then be taken to the police mortuary, where an autopsy may be performed. Some form of post mortem autopsy is performed in many cases of unexpected deaths, even if the cause of death seems obvious.

WHAT YOU NEED TO DO

If you already have a funeral home, let the coroner know who they are, and contact your funeral home as well. The coroner will then know who to contact when your loved one is ready to be transferred to the funeral home. A funeral director from your funeral home will go to the police mortuary, fetch your loved one and transfer them directly to the funeral home.

OR

If you do not have a funeral home, decide on which one you want to help you. This will let the coroner know who they should contact when their investigation is complete (see "Choosing a funeral home").

WHAT HAPPENS TO SOMEONE WHEN THEY HAVE AN AUTOPSY?

There may be different surgical investigations performed on different individuals. Sometimes the investigation is very specific and will only be performed in a localized area, where only a small tissue sample from the area of interest is taken for further investigation. Mostly the coroner's investigation includes all of the systems of the body, including the brain. What this means is that your loved one will have a "Y" shaped incision on their front. The tops of the "Y" start at the front of the shoulders, where they angle slightly downwards to meet at the top of the chest. From here the downward incision of the "Y" runs from the top of the chest to just bellow the belly button. This gives the coroner the ability to make a thorough investigation of all the organs of the body to try to establish the cause of your loved one's death. If the coroner needed to investigate the brain, the head will have an incision from behind one ear, over the top of the head to the back of the other ear.

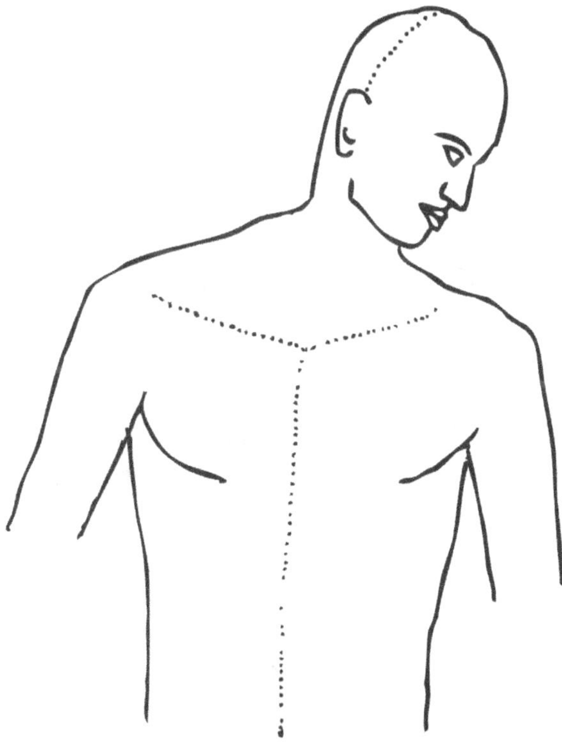

A small tissue sample may be taken from each organ by the coroner, but all of the organs are returned to your loved one.

Their face should look perfectly normal and be unaffected by the autopsy procedure.

I am giving you this information so that you will understand any incisions you may see if you spend time with your loved one at the funeral home after they have been transferred there by your funeral director, and before they have been dressed. Clothes generally cover all of the torso autopsy incisions.

WHAT YOU CAN CHOOSE TO DO

You can have your loved one embalmed.

This makes it possible for you to have more time before their funeral service. If you want to see your loved one, or to have them brought back home as soon as possible, it is important to realize that a person who has had an autopsy may take a lot longer to embalm. The embalmers give each person they work on the unique treatments and procedures that may be required.

OR

You can choose not to have your loved one embalmed.

This can mean that the condition of their body will determine the date for the funeral service, depending on whether you wanted to visit with them in the days before their funeral, or have an open casket at the service.

SPENDING TIME WITH YOUR LOVED ONE AFTER THEY HAVE BEEN AUTOPSIED

You may feel that you said your goodbyes when you last saw them, and you may not want to see them again after their autopsy.

OR

If you would like to see them again before their funeral, you are most welcome to. You may want to help dress them, and you are still able to do so. You can be proactively involved by choosing clothes to cover any evidence there may be of the incisions. For example, by choosing a shirt or blouse that can button up quite high, or using a scarf or cravat to hide any plaster. Bringing a hat or cap can be effective in hiding any evidence of head sutures if your loved one does not have a lot of hair to hide them. Your funeral director will be at your side, helping you and giving you advice through this entire process, should you need it.

NOTES

CHAPTER 4

WHAT OCCURS BIOLOGICALLY TO A BODY WHEN IT DIES

Nature takes its course.
The information in this block is graphic, and it is not essential that you read it. If you are interested in more detail, you may find it informative.

Cultures from around the world have many different views on what happens to a person when they die. These include different beliefs about the person's spirit, soul, mind and body.
I will present to you what happens to a person's body from the moment life leaves it according to modern Western medicine. It is important to note that even from this perspective, death is recognised as being a gradual process and not a sudden event.

Three phases of death have been defined:

1. A doctor or qualified person will declare someone to be **"clinically dead"** when the person has drawn their last breath and their heart is no longer beating. This is the first phase of death. If their heart cannot be massaged to beat again, and their breathing does not resume, this "clinical death" is the stage where the medical personnel declare that there is nothing more that they can do to save the patient, but it does not mean that life has suddenly ended.

2. The lack of oxygen in the blood causes the brain to die, leading to the onset of the second phase of death called **"biological death"**. This is when the organs cease to function.
   It is quite likely that when someone dies, they will still have stored oxygen and nutrients in many of their cells. Metabolic activity will still occur for a while after biological death. Some cells in the body will actually be blissfully unaware that the brain is in fact no longer living and that the heart is no longer beating, and they will continue performing there usual functions until their last spark of energy is used up. You will be able to feel heat radiating from the body of someone who has died as these stores are being used by their body's cells. This can continue for up to six hours. This is why when a person is pronounced dead, many cultures will remain at their loved one's side, and will often not want their body to be disturbed for this time.
3. Eventually these stores will be depleted, and your loved one will go into the third and final stage of death called **"post mortem cellular death"**. This is the age-old process where a body starts to break down at the cellular level. It starts with what is called the "translocation of micro-organisms". This is the movement of micro-organisms from one part of the body to another. Organisms that have a specific function in a particular part of a living body are usually kept in that area by the body's natural defences. When the body goes into "post-mortem cellular death", these organisms can override these defences and move around the body. The main culprits are the micro-organisms of the colon which usually aid us by strengthening our immune system, breaking down our food and helping us with its absorption. During "post-mortem cellular death" these micro-organisms focus their protein, fat and carbohydrate dismantling properties on their host.
   Between 4-8 hours after the time a person is pronounced dead, these micro-organisms have "translocated" into the chambers of the heart, the cerebro-spinal fluid, the lungs and the bladder.

Using these systems of the body as a highway network, they move around the whole body and start dismantling the cells on a chemical level, breaking each cell down into its most basic elements. This process is what we refer to when we speak of a body decomposing.

Rigor mortis can be described as a chemical change that happens in the muscles of someone after they have died. The muscles are unable to complete their normal contraction and release function. As a result they set the limbs of the dead person in a fixed position, making joints stiff and difficult to move. The onset of rigor mortis can start setting in from around three hours after someone has died, and will reach maximum stiffness after twelve hours. Once this point is reached however, rigor mortis gradually releases its hold on the body, but it may still be another two and a half days until the limbs are totally lose.

NOTES

CHAPTER 5

EMBALMING

I am writing about embalming from a New Zealand perspective, where it is quite widely accepted as the standard care given to the body of someone who has died. The ability of the embalming process to radically slow down the natural decomposition of a body when it dies, has contributed a great deal to its popularity and acceptance in this country.

WHY HAVE SOMEONE YOU LOVE EMBALMED?

The three main goals of embalming

1. To sanitize a dead person's body for the protection of their family, friends and society at large from bacteria and diseases associated with dead bodies.

2. To dramatically slow down decomposition, thereby giving the family and friends more time to arrange the funeral.

3. To make the person who has died look peaceful.

The aesthetic goal of embalming is not to have someone appear in a life-like state, but rather to remove as much visible evidence of any trauma from their body as possible. This may have been caused by long-term illness, surgery, trauma or changes that happened to their body after death.

WHERE DOES WESTERN EMBALMING COME FROM?

What is most commonly understood by embalming is based on a technology that was born out of the American Civil War. So many men died in battle, and their passage home for proper family burial was often a long one. There was an urgent need for an effective method of preserving their bodies. So modern Western embalming was pioneered.

WHAT ACTUALLY HAPPENS DURING EMBALMING?

Embalming is the chemical treatment of a dead human body by an embalmer. Embalming fluid is introduced to the body through the arterial system. It has sanitizing, bacteria destroying and protein binding properties.

As this solution is circulated through every cell of the body, the decomposition process is dramatically slowed, and 99% of all harmful viruses and bacteria are destroyed. This makes an embalmed body safe to come into contact with. The eyes and mouth are closed, and a peaceful appearance is restored to the person's face. It is helpful to the embalmers if they have a photo of the person they are working on to ensure that they make them look as natural as possible. You can give a photo to your funeral director when they come to collect your loved one or when first you see them. The photo will be returned to you later. A photo can often be emailed.

The abdominal cavity is also treated to prevent the bacteria from the digestive system from spreading around the body. The body is then washed and groomed.

The information in this block is graphic, and it is not essential that you read it. If you are interested in more detail, you may find it informative.

WHAT HAPPENS TO SOMEONE WHO HAS DIED AND IS TAKEN TO A MORTUARY?

The person is taken directly from the place they died to the funeral home mortuary.

On arrival, a name tag is placed on their wrist or ankle.

A careful inventory of any jewellery and clothes that they are wearing is made and a record kept. If you want a piece of jewellery or a religious adornment to remain with your loved one at all times, be sure to mention this to your funeral director, who will ensure that your wish is carried out. Otherwise all jewellery is removed and safely stored.

The person will be moved from the stretcher onto the embalming table. The embalmer will carefully assess the condition of their body, and decide on the appropriate treatments.

The embalmers will try to ensure that the person they are caring for has a natural and peaceful facial expression. Their hair is also washed and set in their natural style. Other grooming will include thoroughly washing the body, cleaning the nails and any other personal touches (e.g. shaving).

REFRIGERATION AS AN ALTERNATIVE TO EMBALMING AS A MEANS OF PRESERVING A BODY

Some people would prefer their loved one not to be embalmed. It is possible for a body to be kept in a cool room at a funeral home mortuary to preserve them over the short term. This cooling can buy the family a few days if the body is not showing any signs of advancing decomposition. Anyone wanting to visit their loved one should do so sooner rather than later. Decomposition can be delayed by this cooling, but their body is still quite vulnerable to some rapid changes which can gain momentum with varying speeds, depending on each case. What this means is that the person would need to stay in the care of the funeral home until the day of their funeral. Family and friends are able to visit their loved one as often as they want to. The person being visited would be taken out of the cool room and transferred to a private room for each visit, after which they would be returned to the cool room. Certain illnesses or conditions would make this an inadequate method for the effective and safe preservation of the body in some cases, even for a short time. I recommend that you follow your funeral director's advice in this regard.

NOTES

CHAPTER 6

CHOOSING CLOTHES FOR YOUR LOVED ONE

Choosing the clothes that your loved one will wear is a very intimate and personal act. Give yourself time to do this, and ask for the support of someone to do this with you if you think you might need it. By choosing the clothes before your funeral director meets with you, you will be ready to hand them over then. You will not have to suddenly think about which clothes to choose and possibly rush through this process during the meeting. If you don't feel ready to do this yet, tell your funeral director that you will have the clothes ready for them the next day.

The dressing itself can be done by you with your funeral director to assist you, or by your funeral director.

Here are some things to consider when choosing clothes:

- Would you like your loved one to be dressed in their favourite comfy home clothes or something more formal? Sometimes what can have some bearing on this decision is whether you are going to have them visited by family and friends. How would you like them to look? What are you comfortable with? How do you feel your loved one would be comfortable appearing?

- When choosing an outfit for someone, consider what might cover any bruising you may have noticed and do not want to be easily visible (e.g. A long sleeved shirt or blouse, a shawl, long trousers etc). Some health conditions can leave the skin and underlying veins fragile and easily bruised. This can be exacerbated by the administration of medicines through intravenous drips in the arms or legs prior to their death.

- Something to keep in mind is that the embalmers may need to access the carotid artery as the point of applying embalming fluid to the body. This area is located to the side and at the base of the neck. The resulting incision will be small and neatly sutured, usually making it very discreet. Collared shirts for men and high-neckline outfits for ladies cover any slight evidence of the small incision completely, but some T-shirts or more dainty ladies' outfits do not cover this area. If you would like your loved one to wear this type of outfit, a scarf, shawl or silk wrap can be very effective in covering this part of the neck, and can even compliment the outfit. This allows family and friends to focus on the person and not on any concerns over what has been done to their loved one since their death.

- It is a good idea to provide underwear. Shoes and socks are also welcome. Don't forget a belt if the outfit requires one.

- You may want to include some special, personal things (e.g. an item from their hobby, glasses that they always used to wear and fall asleep wearing, a hearing aid, a favourite radio, crossword books, a pet's ashes, etc). Things like these can be worn by the person, or be placed with them in their casket. If you want your loved one to wear a favourite ring, watch, pair of earrings, etc, you can either give them to your funeral director when you see them, or you can bring them with you when you come to visit your loved one, and place these items on them yourself.

CLOTHING & OTHER ITEMS CHECKLIST

____

____

____

____

____

____

____

____

____

____

____

____

CHOOSING TO BE INVOLVED WITH THE DRESSING OF YOUR LOVED ONE

More and more people want to be involved in this dressing ritual. Some people have been caring for and looking after their loved one for some time, and they are very comfortable with and capable of dressing them. Some people on the other hand may be a little nervous to begin with, but when they see how much help and guidance they get with the dressing, they quickly become more relaxed. If this is something new to you, know that you can be involved to whatever degree you choose. You may just wish to be present while they are being dressed. Dressing and visiting someone who has died is a situation where your love and respect for them is often being pulled in the opposite direction by the natural fear and repulsion we humans feel towards dead bodies. It is important to recognise that this internal tug of war is perfectly normal. People deal with death in different ways. It is important that you deal with the death of your loved one in a way that makes sense to you, and that you can cope with. A competent funeral director can be a real anchor at this time. We are there for you exactly because moments like these may be difficult. When you have finished dressing your loved one, you may want to spend some private time with them to fully absorb the experience that you have just shared. You will have prepared them for the next step in their funeral process.

WHEN YOU ARRIVE TO DRESS YOUR LOVED ONE:

- Choose a place where all the people who want to take part can meet. It can be at one of your houses, a coffee shop or at the funeral home. If you choose to meet at the funeral home and some of the group are a bit late, the others in your party might have to wait there and feel a little uneasy. It is good to be a comfortable team when you arrive.

- Bring all the clothes inside with you. Your funeral director will meet you and take you through to their dressing-room where your loved one will be lying on a special dressing table. They will be covered with a white sheet up to their shoulders. On seeing your loved one, you may want a moment of privacy before starting to dress them. Ask your funeral director for this time if you need it. When you are ready to begin, call your funeral director back so that they can guide you through what happens next.

- Lay out all of the clothes you have brought. If you have a few outfits, that's okay. You may decide when you are there which one you want them to wear. You will start with the underwear, and your funeral director will guide you through all of the ways of putting the different layers of clothing on. Get as involved as you are comfortable with.

- It is important to realize that your loved one may have conditions that make their skin delicate, or where care should be taken not to put pressure on their abdominal cavity. Follow the advice and accept the assistance of your funeral director in this regard. We are there to help you. The secret to a successful dressing is 'SLOWLY, SLOWLY'. There is no need to rush - little by little you will get your loved one dressed and looking good.

ONCE YOUR LOVED ONE IS DRESSED:

WHAT YOU CAN CHOOSE TO DO

You can fix their hair and apply their make-up or nail polish on the dressing table once they are dressed, and have your funeral director place them in their casket later, when you have gone.

OR

You can be involved with placing them into their casket.

This is a powerful and special moment, and it is your right as the close family or friend to be involved. Once your loved one is in their casket, you can start 'fine-tuning' the outfit to look natural, well-fitting and flattering. This is the last time they will be moved, so now is the best time to do this. This involves pulling shirts, jerseys and jackets down, especially at the back, getting outfits straightened, and the tucking of any loose material. Then you can fix their hair and apply make-up or nail polish if you want to.

Many family and friends have chatted, laughed and cried as they dressed and groomed their loved one together. Take all the time you need.

Dressing your loved one is intimate. I encourage you to participate in it to whatever degree you feel comfortable with.

NOTES

CHAPTER 7

VISITING SOMEONE AT A FUNERAL HOME

Some people I have talked to while making funeral arrangements, have told me of a negative experience they have had while visiting with someone they cared about who had died. A common complaint was that the person did not look like themselves at all. I can see how this would be upsetting. Embalming has changed a lot over the past two decades. Products and procedures have been refined and improved. However, I can understand the person who says that they have said their last goodbyes to their loved one when they were alive, possibly at their bedside. Some people are very comfortable with that decision.

Sometimes though, a person can linger in a pre-death state for days, and their facial features may distort with pain and their expression can be very distressing to look at. The eyes are often slightly open when someone dies, and the jaw muscles slacken, causing the mouth to open. This last image can be a difficult one to keep as your final one. This is why seeing the peaceful, pain free expression of your loved one can be a tangible and reassuring memory for you, and you can know that the person you care for is no longer in any discomfort and is at peace.

Some people that have not seen their loved one for a long time, or who were not with them when they died, do desperately want to see them one last time, but are also very nervous and might be negative about seeing them. As I have mentioned before, there is a vicious tug of war between the fear and revulsion that most of us feel towards death, and the love and affection we feel for the person who has died. Most people I have seen that did come to spend time with their loved one have been very happy that they did. Many have thanked me for having their loved one ready and looking so peaceful.

CIRCUMSTANCES THAT COULD MAKE SPENDING TIME WITH YOUR LOVED ONE DIFFICULT

There are circumstances however, where visiting someone can be more difficult. If the cause of death has resulted in parts of their body being visibly marked or damaged, or if someone is discovered some days after they have died, when decomposition may be advanced, close family and friends will need to meet with their funeral director and make some informed decisions. In some cases, embalming cannot pull someone's body back from the hold of advanced decomposition. Their body can be sanitized and stabilized, but colour changes and evidence of the body's tissues being broken down may still be evident. Your funeral director will prepare you for what the embalmers have done, and what your loved one will look like if you choose to see them. Badly marked limbs or parts of their body might be bandaged or have some make-up applied to the area. Choosing clothing to specifically hide any area of concern is a good way to proactively deal with this situation. Something as simple as a long-sleeved top can transform the way someone looks.

There are some instances though, where you may be advised not to see your loved one, due to their appearance. This is only advice, and some people have still insisted on seeing them, as is their right. It has at times been upsetting for them, but still positive because it is so personal. They were still able to have that special moment with the person they love. Being prepared for what to expect, what the embalmers have done and why, goes a long way to helping you push through a difficult personal barrier.

Most people who are embalmed appear natural and peaceful. One of the realities of seeing someone who has died is that it provides an opportunity on a sensory and tactile level to overcome any denial there may be of the person's death. This may be a case of what you *need to* experience and do rather than what you *want to* experience or do. Human grief needs a tangible, clear image to focus on, and you will need to decide what feels right for you personally. An embalmer in most cases can serve you by having your loved one looking peaceful and natural. This may create a platform for those who need it to have their "moment of awareness" of the reality of their loved one's death. Some research has shown that those who do visit their loved one are less likely to have unsettled dreams about them later.

SOME HELPFUL THINGS TO BRING WHEN YOU COME TO VISIT YOUR LOVED ONE

There are some tools which may make this private time with the person you love more meaningful and personal.

- You might want to write them a letter or card, which you can slip into an envelope and tuck into their hand or pocket.

- You may want to place some things in their casket with them. Favourite blankets, gadgets or toys, CDs, pictures, drawings, some food or drink. A friendly request however from all crematoriums regarding those who are going to be cremated is that no objects containing batteries be placed in the casket (e.g. cell phones or radios), as the batteries may explode and damage the cremator. These items can still be placed in their casket if the batteries are removed. Another request is that no glass objects be placed in the casket (e.g. bottles of beverage or ornaments), as the glass melts and sticks to the surfaces in the cremator.

If you are nervous about seeing your loved one, tell your funeral director, and they will help and support you until you feel more comfortable. It is a good idea to book a time with your funeral home to come and visit your loved one.

NOTES

CHAPTER 8

HAVING YOUR LOVED ONE BROUGHT BACK TO YOUR HOME

If you have decided to have your loved one brought back to your home until their funeral, your funeral director will assist you with everything to make this possible. We are trained to get a casket into a house in a dignified manner and extra help will be provided should it be needed. If someone is in a casket that is larger than standard-size, it may be difficult to get into a house with tight corners or narrow doors. Try to decide on an area in the house for your loved one that has easy access. Once in your house, a trolley will be provided to place the casket on, which makes moving the casket into the best position very easy.

CARING FOR YOUR LOVED ONE AT HOME

1. Have your loved one placed in a shady room, and not in direct sunlight, or in a room which has a "greenhouse", hot and muggy feel to it. You should not put a heater on in the room. The room does not need to be extremely cold either, normal room temperature is fine. A body's temperature will attune to the room's temp. This should be allowed to happen.

2. A net or sheet should be placed over the casket if they are left unattended at any time. Flies are not particularly attracted to an

embalmed body, but they might land on your loved one, just as they might land on you or me, though we will wave them away.

3. When a person dies, their skin is no longer being moistened by naturally secreted oils, and the surrounding air slowly takes moisture from it each day. When someone has been cared for by a funeral home, the embalmer puts a barrier moisturiser onto the skin wherever it is exposed to the air to prevent this moisture loss. This helps prevent the skin from darkening because of dehydration. This should be adequate protection for your loved one at home. There are some instances however when many people have touched the hands and kissed and touched the face of the person who has died, when a light layer of very simple moisturiser should be reapplied to the face and hands. If you are concerned that you have put too much on, you may gently dab the face and hands with a clean, soft cloth until you feel you have restored a more natural look to their skin.

It is perfectly normal for an embalmed body to have a slight chemical smell to it. Some people have placed the lid back on the casket at night, when all windows and doors of the house have been closed for the evening. Some people have burned incense or aromatherapy oils to mask the smell, and some have chosen to use a favourite perfume or after shave. I must caution you against applying any perfumes directly to the skin though, for example on the face or neck areas. Some chemical compounds in the perfume may dehydrate and darken any skin that they come into contact with. You can apply perfume to your loved one's clothing or to tissues that can be tucked behind the side curtaining of the casket. It is better to be prepared for this so that if you do choose to bring your loved one home, you are comfortable with anything that you may encounter.

You will have your funeral director's contact details if you have any concerns at all.

NOTES

CHAPTER 9

MEETING WITH THE FUNERAL DIRECTOR

On calling your funeral home, a funeral director will answer any immediate questions you may have about your loved one. They will then confirm a time and venue of your choosing to have this meeting with you. In this meeting they will get all of the necessary information from you to legally register your loved one's death. This enables them to apply for a death certificate for your loved one on your behalf. They will also plan the actual funeral service with you, including what you would like to happen in the days leading up to it.

Each funeral home will have their own forms and formats, but I will give you the general information they will want from you, so you can be better prepared and possibly have time to discuss some points with family and friends beforehand. This prevents any "on the spot" decisions which you may make while not in a clear head space because of grief, but which you may have changed in hind sight.

Remember there is no need to rush through this meeting. As funeral directors we are prepared to work through each point until we have all the information we need to ensure your loved one's funeral goes according to your wishes. Each arrangement will be unique, unfolding in its own time, in its own way, so do not feel pressured.

You are welcome to have as many people present as you would like for support and input, or you may prefer to meet with your funeral director on your own.

INFORMATION REQUIRED FOR THE DEATH CERTIFICATE:

Personal information of the person who has died:

- Full name
- Gender
- Date of birth
- Place of birth
- Usual residence
- Phone number
- Occupation
- How many years they have lived in the country
- If they were ever a serviceman or servicewoman:
- Service no: Rank: Regiment:
- Married/Never married Defacto/Civil Union
- Name of husband/wife/partner
- Age of husband/wife/partner if still living
- If married, where?

- Age of the person who has died when they got married

- Widow/Widower Divorced/Separated

- Age of living biological children

Family information of the person who has died:

- Father's name

- Father's occupation

- Mother's name

- Mother's maiden name

- Mother's occupation

NOTES

PLANNING THE FUNERAL

Do not let the underlying headings make you feel pressured to include them all. Use only what feels right.

There are three important pillars upon which the funeral is built:

WHERE, WHEN, and WHO?

1) **Where would you like the funeral service to be held?**

A funeral can be held anywhere. This can be inside a building, or outside in nature. When choosing to have an inside funeral, you need to be sure that the venue is available on the day and at the time of your choosing. An outside funeral in a garden or on a beach does not normally have those constraints, but other factors like the weather and the quality of the terrain for elderly guests or for pall bearing need to be kept in mind.

2) **On what day and at what time would you like to have the funeral service?**

Each family will want the funeral to be on a date that gives enough time for them to contact people, allows for travel time, and also allows time for anyone who wants to visit with their loved one in the days leading up to the funeral service. Family and friends may also have chosen to be involved, and will need time to perform tasks like:

- Going through pictures for a picture board or a DVD presentation for the service.

OR

- Choosing the right music to be played at different times in the service.

Some family and friends may also want to take over some of the tasks ordinarily done by the funeral director (e.g. the designing and printing of the service sheets or organizing the flowers for the casket).

For some families, circumstances out of their control make it impossible to choose the exact funeral date and time. Overseas relatives may need to be contacted and notified that a loved one has died, and sometimes this can take days or even weeks. Some countries also take longer to grant travel visas to those who wish to attend the funeral service. If you think this could be the case, then let your funeral director know as soon as possible so that they can support you in your process. This will impact on how they care for your loved one's body over this time.

3) Who would you like to lead the funeral service for you?

This can be a member of the clergy, a celebrant, and even a friend or member of the family. Some families have very specific requests or arrangements with regard to who leads their loved one's funeral service. This may be because they attended a funeral where they liked the way someone led a service, or it may be a family friend or contact who knew the person who has died. Many families have expressed how much they would like to have someone who knew the person to lead the service. Sadly this is not always possible. Do not be concerned if you find this to be your situation. Your funeral director will have many male and female celebrants and members of the clergy who they often work with. They will be able to suit someone to your loved one's personality and interests. This "picture" of your loved one that your funeral director will get during your meeting will help them in choosing the best suited person to help you. They will let you know the name of the person the moment that they have confirmed that they are available on the day of the funeral service. The nominated person will contact you to make a time to meet, to talk about the person who has died and to get any other information that they might need. Celebrants are always helpful and supportive in offering guidance and advice, for instance when a song might be sung or an instrumental piece played. They are also able to tactfully handle any sensitive family situations that may be an issue.

With these three tiers of the service in place, the funeral has a definite form which allows the close family and friends to answer the questions that might be asked of them by all those wishing to attend the funeral.

A newspaper notice including all of the funeral details can now be safely placed if you wish to have one, however it is not compulsory.

NOTES

PLACING A NEWSPAPER NOTICE

WHAT YOU CAN CHOOSE TO DO

Your funeral director can place the notice on your behalf.

You can have something written down and ready to give to them when they meet with you, or you can work through the notice wording with them during the meeting. Apart from needing to start with the persons name, it can be formal or informal.

OR

You can place the newspaper notice privately yourself.

You can do this by email or by phone. If you choose to do this, check with whichever newspaper you would like to place the notice in as to when there cut-off time is for publishing on the following day. Some newspapers close on Saturdays and open for a few hours on Sunday afternoon for the Monday publication.

Some wording ideas for a newspaper notice:

- Much loved
- Beloved
- Loved and adored
- Cherished
- loved and respected
- husband/wife, best friend and soul mate of _____

If you are looking for more ideas in regard to wording, read some other notices in the newspaper.

Some ideas for wording the funeral details:

A funeral service for________________ will be held at __________________ on the ____ of _________ at _____am/pm.

When It's Time to Call the Funeral Director

If you don't have all the funeral details when you want to place the notice, you can simply end the notice with "details to follow" or "all communications to (phone number)".

If your loved one is going to be home for people to visit in the days before their funeral, do not give your home address in the notice. You can say, "(name) will be lying in state at home", or less formally, "all are welcome to visit (name) at his home". (Some opportunists may take advantage of the empty house at the time of the funeral service).

NOTES

CHOOSING A CASKET

Choosing a casket for someone is a very personal thing. I have seen this decision placed solely on one person and sometimes family and friends make this decision together.

WHAT YOU CAN CHOOSE TO DO

You can make the casket yourself.

If you have the skill and the desire, this can be a very practical and personal way of being involved in your loved one's funeral. If they are to be cremated, your funeral director will be able to get you the guidelines to ensure that all materials used are within acceptable crematorium emission protocols. There are many helpful books and websites in this regard.

OR

You can purchase a casket through your funeral home.

Your funeral director will usually present you with a picture catalogue of caskets, but some funeral homes have a room where caskets are viewable for those who need to see and touch them to feel that they are making the right choice.

A casket ultimately houses your loved one's body. What a casket is made of, decorative detail and craftsmanship is what adds to the cost. You can personalise a ready made casket with paint, stickers, written messages or in any other way that you can imagine.

Go into the arrangement with an idea of what you would like to spend on a casket. Make a decision that you are totally comfortable with. Do not be pressurized into spending more than you would have wanted to because of an awkward family dynamic or because of the emotionally charged climate of the meeting.

NOTES

WOULD YOU LIKE THERE TO BE CASKET BEARERS?

There is place for six casket bearers. Most bearers are surprised at how light their loved one feels. If you take their weight and divide it by six, it seldom works out to be more than 15kg - 20kg per bearer. Most healthy, active people and even older children can cope with this load comfortably. People with a large family and several friends usually have no difficulty in having very willing casket bearers volunteer. Young children are welcome to walk alongside or to place a hand on the casket to be a part of the casket bearing.

If however, you would very much like there to be casket bearers but you are concerned that the person who has died has very few friends and family, or perhaps most of those who will be attending the funeral might be too frail, this does not mean that you will not be able to have their casket carried. Your funeral director will be able to arrange casket bearers for you.

There is also the option of the casket being easily moved on a casket trolley with as few as two people. The casket will effectively be on castor wheels, and the motion is therefore very smooth.

NOTES

WOULD YOU LIKE THE CASKET TO BE OPEN OR CLOSED AT THE FUNERAL SERVICE?

WHAT YOU CAN CHOOSE TO DO

You can have the casket closed at the service.

Sometimes people will arrive early to place flowers on or near the casket, or perhaps just to touch it out of love and respect for the person who has died. In this case, you might like there to be a casket photo of your loved one on top of the casket lid. This can be a framed picture that you already have at home, or there may be a smaller photo that you want your funeral director to enlarge and have framed for you. This also provides the opportunity at the end of the service for those gathered to place a farewell tribute around this picture, instead of on the plain casket surface.

Sometimes there is pressure from people who are far away and are not able to come to view their loved one immediately. They may still want to see them a last time at the funeral service. There are different ways to have an open casket at the funeral, perhaps a way can be found that the family will be comfortable with.

Following are some possibilities:

You may wish to have an open casket for a short time before the service.

The casket can be in place and open at the front of the funeral venue, and those wanting to see the person a last time must come early to do so. The casket can then be closed by your funeral director a few minutes before the service is to start. The casket would remain closed from this point onward.

OR

You may wish to have an open casket for the duration of the funeral service.

The casket would stay open until the agreed-upon time in the service. Your funeral director would then come forward to close the casket for the last time.

NOTES

WOULD YOU LIKE THERE TO BE FLOWERS ON THE CASKET AND AT THE FUNERAL VENUE?

WHAT YOU CAN CHOOSE TO DO

You can arrange for the flowers yourself.

This is often an area where someone in the family or a close friend would like to get involved. Flowers can be picked from your own garden if this has significance, or arranged through a florist.

OR

You can have your funeral director arrange for the flowers for you.

We have many florists who deliver fresh arrangements exactly as ordered. Looking at pictures of flower arrangements can be helpful when choosing a style, whether it is for the casket or for a supporting arrangement that would be placed near the casket.

NOTES

PLACING A FAREWELL TRIBUTE ON THE CASKET AT THE END OF THE SERVICE

You may like to place flower petals or flower heads on your loved one's casket as a final farewell at the end of the service.

You are not restricted to these two options. You can use leaves, glitter, or anything you feel is relevant to your loved one.

If this farewell is going to take place at the hearse, it is a good idea to have something a little heavier to place which may be better able to stay on the casket in case of any wind that could blow lighter things away as people are placing them. For indoor farewell tributes or outdoors at the graveside, anything that you decide upon would be fine.

Balloons or doves too can be released as another symbolic act of saying goodbye.

NOTES

OTHER THINGS YOUR FUNERAL DIRECTOR MAY ASK YOU:

WOULD YOU LIKE TO HAVE A PRE-FUNERAL FAMILY SERVICE?

This is a way to honour and respect your loved one in a context different from a formal funeral service. It can happen on a day before the funeral, where family and friends can gather at a venue of their choosing, from a home to a sports club. Your loved one's body can be present, but doesn't need to be.

WHAT YOU WILL NEED TO DO

Choose a venue, the day and time that you would like the family service to be held on, and if you would like your loved one to be there, your funeral director will arrange for this.

This service can be held in whichever format you prefer. At the end of the service, family and friends may want a time of sharing together over refreshments.

If your loved one was present, at a time agreed upon, they would be taken back to the funeral home, or returned to your home if that is where you wanted them to be.

NOTES

WOULD YOU LIKE A DVD RECORDING OF THE FUNERAL SERVICE?

You may like a DVD recording of the funeral service to keep, or to send a copy to someone who was overseas or who simply was not able to attend the funeral service on the day, though they desperately wanted to. They too can hear the eulogy, the other tributes given, the music chosen and belatedly experience the funeral service wherever they are. Even though it would not be in real time, they can still feel part of the funeral of their loved one, and hopefully it would help them in their grieving process.

Some chapel facilities have a recording system already set up, but some venues would require someone to arrange for this.

WHAT YOU CAN CHOOSE TO DO

You can record the funeral service yourself.

A family member or friend may volunteer to record the service for the family. This can be out of a desire to give love and support in a tangible way and possibly to save the family the cost of hiring someone else. This is welcome, but I have seen how performing this task can sometimes cause the person doing the recording to not be completely "in" the service. They are understandably very concerned with making the best recording that they can. It may be worth getting someone who is not very close to the person who has died to do this recording, or consider hiring a professional camera person if you are able to, thereby allowing all of those personally affected by the death of their loved one to be focused solely on the funeral service and to grieve without distraction.

OR

You can have your funeral director arrange for the recording of the service for you.

NOTES

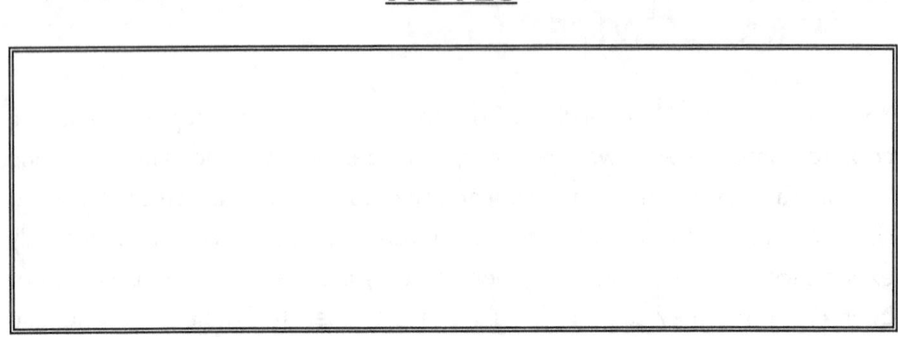

HOW WOULD YOU LIKE THE FUNERAL SERVICE TO END?

POSSIBLE BURIAL SERVICE ENDINGS

If you have chosen for your loved one to be buried, here are the different possibilities regarding what happens once the casket bearers have placed their casket over the grave.

Using a lowering device

A lowering device is a mechanical means of lowering a casket into a grave. The lowering action is very gradual and smooth. The casket bearers' responsibility would be to carry the casket from the hearse to the grave where your funeral director and cemetery staff will guide them in placing the casket safely onto the straps of the lowering device.

The lowering device would be activated at the instruction of the person taking the service when it is time.

WHAT YOU CAN CHOOSE TO DO

You or a nominated person can activate the lowering device.

There is absolutely nothing preventing any family member or friend from activating the lowering device themselves. Your funeral director will simply show that person how it operates before the graveside service begins.

OR

You can have your funeral director activate the lowering device for you.

Once your loved one's casket is resting at the bottom of the grave, farewell tributes can be dropped onto it. You can leave the graveside whenever you feel ready to.

Some families choose to fill the grave in themselves. Shovels can be arranged for you if this is something you would like to do. It can be muddy work, especially if it has been raining, so bring a pair of gumboots for this part of the service. You may choose to fill the grave just enough to cover the casket, or you may want to fill the grave completely, after which someone will push the grave cross or marker into the soft earth at the head side of the grave.

Using sticks and straps

Two thick planks would be in place across the grave, onto which the casket bearers would place the casket. Three thick nylon straps or ropes would be in place for the lowering of the casket.

At a signal from the person leading the graveside service, your funeral director will step forward and invite the casket bearers to take their positions alongside the casket. The six bearers will take hold of the straps or ropes, thread them through the casket handles, and lift the casket off of the planks. Your funeral director will pull the planks out from under the casket, allowing the bearers to slowly lower the casket.

Sometimes families express concern over the weight of the casket and possible slipperiness of the straps if it were to rain. It is important to remember that the load on each casket bearer is usually less than 20kg, making this a very possible and tactile way of lowering your loved one's casket to their final resting place. Even in the rain, I have never seen anyone have the straps slip through their grip. If anyone was battling with the weight at any time in the lowering, remember there are four other bearers who would absorb what they were unable to bear.

Once your loved one's casket is resting at the bottom of the grave, farewell tributes can be dropped onto it. When you feel ready, you can leave the graveside or stay to fill it in if you wish.

Choosing not to lower the casket while you are there

The lowering of the casket at a burial service is not compulsory. The casket bearers can place the casket over the grave on the straps of the lowering device, and let it remain like that for the duration of the graveside committal service.

When it comes to the end of the service, you could place your farewell tribute on top of your loved one's casket, and when you feel ready to leave, you can do so. The casket will not be lowered with the family there. The cemetery staff would wait for everyone to have left the area before they lower your loved one's casket and filled the grave in.

NOTES

Some practical considerations when attending a burial

If there is the possibility of rain, take a raincoat or umbrella. Flat-soled shoes can also make it safer to walk over any uneven ground, especially if you are a casket bearer.

If you have chosen for your loved one to be buried and you already have a plot at a cemetery

Your funeral director will want the cemetery and burial plot details. This is to enable them to book a burial time with that cemetery according to the time and date of the funeral service.

If you do not have a burial plot, do not be concerned. Your funeral director will book your cemetery of choice to ensure that the burial will happen after the service. They will then arrange for you to go to the cemetery to choose and purchase a plot. Your funeral director will process all of the paperwork required.

Things to consider when purchasing a burial plot

When you purchase a burial plot at a cemetery, you are not purchasing the land, but rather the right to have someone interred in that piece of land. The burial rights to any unused plot belong to the purchaser for a period of sixty years or more, depending on each cemetery. If no one is interred in a pre-purchased plot within this period, the purchaser is given first option to repurchase the burial rights of any unused plot, thereby renewing the agreement for another sixty-plus years.

Once someone is interred in a plot, they will not be disturbed again. The burial rights to that plot from now on belong to the purchaser. Any changes to the headstone or additional interments into that plot will need the permission and signature of the person who bought the burial rights for it.

Some cemeteries allow many burial plots to be bought in close proximity to each other. This allows family members or friends to know that they will all be close together when they die and are interred. I mention this now, as I have assisted some families who have had trouble obtaining a plot close to where a family member had been interred some years previously. They often have to settle on the closest available plot. There is the obvious expense involved in this for the family, but if this might be important to you, it is better to be aware of this now.

Once you have purchased a plot, you can also choose whether you would like the grave to be dug to a single or double interment depth. A double-depth grave means that two people can be interred in the same plot. The first person being interred will be slightly deeper, to be followed later by a single-depth grave re-opening at the time when the second person is to be interred. This saves the family the expense of purchasing two plots, and only the single-depth re-opening fee would apply for the second interment.

NOTES

BURIAL AT SEA

There are specially designated areas off the coastline, well clear of any fishing grounds, where sea burials are allowed. If you wanted your loved one to be buried at sea, your funeral director would get the necessary permission from the local coroner and maritime authorities.

Transferring your loved one to your chosen sea burial area can be done with your own ocean-going vessel, or by hiring one. Some families have even chosen to hire a helicopter. On choosing the size of vessel, consider the number of people you wish to attend the sea burial. If hiring a larger vessel is too costly, an alternative might be to have a land-based funeral service for your loved one, which many people could attend, after which a small group of family and friends would follow the hearse to a smaller ocean-going vessel, where only they would attend the sea burial. It may take some hours to get to the sea burial area, and you can be on the water for half of the day.

It is important to know that if the skipper feels that the weather at the planned time of departure is going to make the outing unsafe, they may postpone the trip until the weather has calmed.

NOTES

POSSIBLE CREMATION SERVICE ENDINGS

This is the moment of final farewell. A moment you will carry in your memory to look back on for the rest of your life.

If you have chosen for your loved one to be cremated, here are the different possibilities as to how their funeral service can end:

Leaving the casket in place at the end of the service

If the service is held at a crematorium chapel, at the conclusion of the service your loved one's casket would remain in place. There is usually a button that the person leading the service can activate to lower the casket in a symbolic way. You can decide whether or not you want their casket to be lowered at all. In many crematorium chapels, the casket will not disappear from sight, and will only be lowered a short distance. The person taking the service would then invite the family first, then friends, to come forward to place a farewell tribute on the casket. There is no need to rush this at all, so take as much time at your loved one's casket as you need. When you are ready to leave, you would exit the venue and go to the pre-arranged refreshment venue for a further time of sharing and touching-down with all of those who have come to the funeral. When everyone has left the service venue, the crematorium staff will discreetly transfer your loved one from the chapel to the crematorium.

OR

If the service is held at a venue away from the crematorium, you can still choose to have your loved one stay in place at the close of the service. The person taking the service would invite the family first, then friends, to come forward to place a farewell tribute on their casket. When everyone has left the service venue to meet over refreshments, your funeral director will discreetly take your loved one to the crematorium.

NOTES

Casket bearing your loved ones casket to the hearse

If the service is held away from the crematorium, at a sign from the person leading the service that it has ended, your funeral director will have your chosen casket bearing music play, come forward, and invite the bearers to do the same. The casket bearers would take their places at the casket and carry your loved one out to the hearse. The rest of the family will follow, then the rest of the congregation.

At the hearse your loved one's casket will be placed part-way into the vehicle, leaving a part easily accessible for anyone wishing to place a farewell tribute on it. When everyone who has wanted to place a tribute has done so, your funeral director will secure your loved one's casket in the hearse and close the back hatch. They will let you know that they are going to leave for the crematorium shortly. While everyone is still gathered, the hearse will slowly drive away, with everyone watching its departure.

Some members of the family and close friends may want to go with their loved one to the crematorium immediately after the service, but express concern over not wanting to split the group of people that have gathered for the funeral. This concern can be addressed in the following ways:

The hearse does not have to leave for the crematorium immediately. Once the casket bearers have placed your loved one in the hearse, the hearse can stay in place until the important time with friends and family during refreshments is over. When most people have left the gathering, the close group of family and friends who want to go with their loved one to the crematorium can do so.

OR

If you are not comfortable with the idea of your loved one being left in the hearse for the refreshment time, another possibility is that at the conclusion of the service their casket would remain in place at the front of the service venue. At the end of the service, farewell tributes would still be placed on their casket, after which every one would exit the venue, following the family into a refreshment area for that special time of togetherness. When most of the gathered people have left, the close group of family and friends would make their way back into the service venue, where they would casket bear their loved one to the hearse, and then escort them to the crematorium.

NOTES

A crematorium escort and farewell

Some families struggle over whether or not to go with their loved one to the crematorium at all. "It would be like having the funeral service all over again," is something I have heard expressed. If you feel really divided over this, consider simply driving behind the hearse to the crematorium, and then peeling away as it enters the crematorium grounds.

If you would like to escort your loved one right to the crematorium and casket bear them the last few metres into a chapel there, here is what you can expect to happen once the convoy has arrived at the crematorium:

When It's Time to Call the Funeral Director

- Your funeral director would have booked a private chapel for you, and will stop the hearse outside its doors. The casket bearers will gather at the hearse and your loved one will be carried into the chapel and placed on the catafalque at the front. This is a raised platform which supports a casket.

- Now it can be helpful if a member of the family or a close friend took the role of "master of ceremonies", albeit in a very personalized and informal way. If you feel that no family member or friend would be up to performing this role on the day, your clergyman or celebrant will gladly do this for you.

- Everyone will gather around the casket and usually remain standing. The "master of ceremonies" would remind everyone why they have gathered, and they might explain to everyone what this time will be used for. They would then invite anyone to say what they perhaps were not comfortable saying during the more crowded main service. An opportunity can be provided for any letters, photos, gifts, flowers or any more farewell tributes to be placed on the casket. These items will stay with your loved one and be cremated with them.

- There could be markers to write messages on the casket, stories could be told or there could just be silence for a time. Perhaps a favourite song could be played over the sound system or sung. Your funeral director will be on hand to make sure this goes as planned.

- One of the most important parts of what the "master of ceremonies" needs to do in this informal service is to bring it to a definite close. With some thought and planning, this personal farewell can create a powerful and beautiful memory. It may well be sad, but appropriately so.

- There is normally a button on the lectern or wall at a crematorium chapel that will activate the lowering of the casket when you press it. Your funeral director will show the "master of ceremonies" where it is. You can decide whether you want your loved one's casket to be lowered at the closure or not. You do not have to have their casket lowered at all.

- If you choose to lower your loved one's casket, it is important to realize that in many chapels, when the lowering button is activated, the casket does not disappear out of sight, but simply lowers a short distance as more of a symbolic act. It is important that you know this, because at a point when the gathering has been concluded, you are going to have to turn around and walk away when you can still see your loved one's casket. It is helpful for family and friends to know that this moment is coming, so that they can support each other through it.

NOTES

ASHES

If you have chosen for your loved one to be cremated, your funeral director will enquire as to what you would like to do with your loved one's ashes.

WHAT YOU CAN CHOOSE TO DO

You can scatter their ashes.

This can be done at a specially chosen place, or at a designated ash scattering area in a cemetery.

OR

You can keep them at home.

OR

You can have them interred (buried).

If you would like to have your loved one's ashes interred, here are some possibilities to consider:

You can inter them at your residence.

Keep in mind the possibility of you moving house one day. If you would want to take them with you in the event of you moving, have them interred in a robust and waterproof urn.

OR

You can lay your loved one's ashes to rest at a cemetery.

If this is what you would like to do, here are some possibilities:

You can purchase an ash plot, and in some cemeteries a wall vault.

OR

If a family member has previously been interred in a casket burial plot, you can have your loved one's ashes interred in that same plot.

This makes it possible for family members to be interred together, even if someone has chosen to be cremated. Some cemeteries allow as many as eight ash interments in a casket burial plot, provided the casket burials have already taken place. This saves you an ash plot

purchase fee, and you will only need to pay the digging fee for each ash interment.
Your funeral director can help you with whatever you have decided.

If you are not yet sure what you are going to do with your loved ones ashes, your funeral director will safely keep them until the time is right and a decision has been made by close family and friends.
Unless you have chosen a particular ash urn that you have given your funeral director, crematoriums generally seal someone's ashes in a rectangular hard plastic container, about the size of half a shoe box. This container is waterproof and very durable. An adult's ashes will weigh between 2 and 4 kilograms.

NOTES

ASH URNS

WHAT YOU CAN CHOOSE TO DO

You do not need to buy a formal ash urn.

You can make a home made one out of wood, clay or any other material you feel would work. You can even buy a decorative container made of copper or glass for example, and devise a nice looking and effective lid for it if it does not have one. For example, a silk scarf can be tightly rolled to make an effective and beautiful stopper. Ask your funeral director for advice regarding the size that a vessel would need to be to hold all of the ashes.

OR

You can ask your funeral director to show you a selection of traditional ash urns for you to choose from.

Your loved one's ashes will usually be ready for collection from the crematorium within 48 hours of their cremation.

WHAT YOU CAN CHOOSE TO DO

You can collect their ashes yourself.

Your funeral director will let the crematorium staff know that you will be coming. Bring your driver's license or some other form of legal identification with you, as they need to ensure that they are handing the ashes to the correct person.

OR

You can have your funeral director collect their ashes on your behalf.

NOTES

WHAT MUSIC WOULD YOU LIKE TO BE PLAYED AT THE FUNERAL SERVICE?

The music you choose for the funeral service provides an opportunity for you to put the personal touch of the person who has died on their funeral service. The following ideas are guidelines, a starting point for you to discuss around, until you are happy with what music will be played and when.

Before the service begins

People will start arriving at a funeral venue from thirty minutes before the service is due to begin, right up to the last minute. It is therefore a good idea to have background music playing during this time. This can be in the form of an organist playing selected pieces, or a compiled CD with about ten tracks recorded. This will create an atmosphere fitting to your loved one's nature and personality.

NOTES

To start the service

You may want to start the service with a special song.

NOTES

During the service

At the point in the service when all tributes have been made, the person taking the service may suggest a time of reflection, during which a specially chosen piece can be played. This can be someone singing, a track from a CD, an organist, a piper, an instrumental piece or anything else you feel would be fitting.

There are still other opportunities during the service if anyone would like to play an instrument or sing a song.

NOTES

At the end of the service

If the casket is to stay in place at the conclusion of the service, a piece of music could play as family and friends come forward to place a farewell tribute on their loved ones casket as a final goodbye.

If the casket is to be taken to the hearse at the conclusion of the service, a chosen piece of music would play as the casket is carried.

The person leading the service, along with your funeral director, will need to know what music you want to be played and when. It is a good idea to drop off any music and DVD presentations with your funeral director at least a day before the service, so that they can test them all on the service venue's sound and DVD equipment.

NOTES

WOULD YOU LIKE THERE TO BE A SERVICE SHEET?

A service sheet will often have a picture of the person who has died on the front cover with their name, and the dates of their birth and death. You are welcome to include other photos on the inside or on the back page of the service sheet.

Inside will be the funeral service details which will include the venue, the date and time of the service, and the minister or celebrant's name. One of the functions of the service sheet is to have the words of any hymns, poems, songs, passage of scripture or piece of literature printed for those attending the funeral to follow.

WHAT YOU CAN CHOOSE TO DO

You can make the service sheets yourself.

This is another task that some families and friends may choose to take on.

OR

You can have your funeral director make the service sheets.

When It's Time to Call the Funeral Director

Your funeral director will collect any pictures and service sheet content from you. Give them a rough idea of how many people you think might be attending the service, to enable them to print the correct quantity of service sheets for you.

A family member or friend can be nominated to hand these out as people arrive for the service, or your funeral director can do this for you.

NOTES

WOULD YOU LIKE THERE TO BE REFRESHMENTS AFTER THE FUNERAL SERVICE?

After the funeral service, you may want to have a time of sharing and integrating with all of those who have gathered.

WHAT YOU CAN CHOOSE TO DO.

You can arrange the venue and catering yourself.

Some families choose to provide refreshments at somebody's home after the service. Make sure that arranging this does not put too much additional

stress on the family and friends performing this task, as the funeral day is very stressful in itself.
You can privately book a hall, sports club, beach-café or anywhere that you felt would be an appropriate venue.

OR

You can have your funeral director arrange for the refreshments.

Your funeral director will be able to arrange a refreshment area, and caterers who can provide this service for you, even if the funeral is at another venue.

NOTES

WOULD YOU LIKE THERE TO BE A PICTURE BOARD?

If there are going to be refreshments after the funeral, whether at the service venue's refreshment lounge, another venue or someone's home, this may be an opportunity to have a picture board set up. This can be a wonderful focal point. All of the people there can remember and talk about the times and occasions captured in the photos. You can also have a table alongside with some hobby items, art or other personal things of your loved one on display. Those closest to the person who has died, whether on their own or together in a group, can spend some time sorting through items and pictures, and choosing the most appropriate ones. This experience can be emotional and it may be difficult coming to terms with the reality of your loved one having died. This can be a very special time in the days leading up to the funeral.

NOTES

WOULD YOU LIKE TO HAVE A DVD PRESENTATION TO BE PLAYED?

This involves between 50 or 60 pictures which are displayed on a big screen in a chosen sequence, to background music. This DVD can be played before the service begins as people take their seats in the venue, or at another chosen time in the service.

WHAT YOU CAN CHOOSE TO DO

You can make the DVD presentation yourself.

Be sure to test it on the service venues DVD player at least a day before the funeral to make sure that your copy is compatible with the system there.

OR

You can have your funeral director arrange for the DVD presentation to be made.

Give your funeral director all of the photos you have chosen, in the sequence that you want them to be shown in, along with the music you would like to have played during the presentation.

NOTES

WOULD YOU LIKE THERE TO BE A MEMORIAL BOOK?

Having a memorial book on the day of the funeral, gives the people who attend the service an opportunity to record their attendance. Looking back through this record can be helpful to you in the weeks after the funeral if you wanted to send "thank you" cards, or to make contact with some of the people who wrote a message, or simply to know who was there, as the day can pass in a blurr.

WHAT YOU CAN CHOOSE TO DO

You can arrange for your own memorial book.

Some families bring their own "memorial book" on the day of the funeral. This can be a scrapbook, a photo album or something else you would like to use. Often it is the same book that has been in the room of the person who has died while they were unwell. Many friends and family would have already written in it during the days or weeks of visiting with them leading up to their death. This same book may also be placed where they are to be visited in the days leading up to their funeral.

OR

You can have your funeral director arrange for a memorial book.

OR

You can choose not to have a memorial book.

If there is only going to be a small gathering of close friends and family, you may feel no need to have one.

NOTES

CONCLUSION

Do the work in this, your loved one's funeral process. Be patient with yourself. A funeral is something that has many parts to it. You can get involved in as many as you feel comfortable with. Provide yourself with the opportunities you may need to express your love for, and grief over, the one you have lost. Physically mourn in as personal a way as you are able. See opportunity, stay connected, and take courage.

NOTES

PART TWO

Parents and family knowing their rights and the choices available to them will not find this time any easier, but it will make what happens from the time of their baby's death (and how they say goodbye to them) very personal. A big hope of mine is that some people who read this information will be able to pass it on and help anyone they know whose baby is dying or has died.

My heart goes out to any parent who is reading this book because their own baby is dying or has died. No parent should have to endure such a thing.

CHAPTER 10

WHEN A BABY DIES

The term "baby" is used by parents to refer to an embryo, a stillborn foetus, a neonate, a baby and a toddler. I understand this broad use of the term "baby", and this is why in the information that follows I too have used the word "baby" to include all of these instances.
To the medical and legal institutions however, there are very specific terms that define the developmental stages of a human baby:

- From the moment of conception to eight weeks into the pregnancy, a baby is called an embryo.

- From nine weeks into the pregnancy until the moment of birth, a baby is referred to as a foetus.

- From the day of its birth until it has completed its 28th day, the baby is called a neonate.

- From the 29th day of the baby's life outside of the womb until their 1st birthday, they can now officially be called a baby.

- The day after their 1st birthday and continuing until they are 2years old, a baby is called a toddler.

There is one important legal dividing line in these terms which is important for you as a family to know. It has direct bearing on what you are required to do by law following the death of your baby, and what you are allowed to do when planning how you will lay them to rest.

MISCARRIED BABIES

If a baby is miscarried, their death does not need to be registered with the 'Births, Deaths and Marriages' registrar (BDM), and consequently you will not receive a death certificate for them.

LEGAL DEFINITION OF A MISCARRIAGE

In New Zealand, a miscarriage is defined as a pregnancy that ends spontaneously within 20 weeks of the pregnancy having begun, where the foetus is unable to survive. This would include any foetus weighing less than 400g.
It can be difficult to read such a "matter of fact" statement at a time when your baby means so much more to you than facts and definitions. The implications of this definition is that, if your baby is miscarried, you are able to take them home with you as soon as the hospital has given you, the mother, your hospital discharge papers. You do not have to wait for a "cause of death" discharge certificate to be completed by your doctor on behalf of your baby. When a baby is miscarried, the parents and close family are often left devastated. Whether an embryo has miscarried very early in a pregnancy or whether a foetus is stillborn much later, I believe it is important to recognise that the parents are suffering the loss of their baby. For many mums the connection and love for their baby started the moment they realised that a spark of human life had been ignited inside of them. In many cases the mums have said that they knew they were pregnant even before a doctor had confirmed it to them, that they just felt different. Their hope, excitement, anticipation and tenderness quickly ripple through the whole family. All are in awe of one of the most beautiful and powerful experiences of being human. An undeniable love connection can develop between the parents and their baby

in such short a time, and this can result in a very deep grief when their baby miscarries.

A miscarriage is an extremely emotional, delicate and sensitive time for the parents and all of those family and friends closely involved. Different members of this close group will be dealing with the loss of the baby in their own way, and can sometimes become emotionally 'stuck' in their grief for a long time. A grieving platform can be helpful in bringing everyone affected together, to help them move toward a closure over their loss, and its impact on their lives. An informal and personal funeral service can be held for your baby, with their body present at the service, allowing family and friends to share their grief and offer each other support.

If you feel uncomfortable with the idea of taking your baby home, then let me put forward an observation I have made. Many people who have lost a loved one but never got to see their body (for example in an airplane crash or in circumstances of war), have really struggled with their grief because of how important it is for them to have the physical body to "lay to rest". I have spoken with women whose still-born babies had been discreetly removed from the delivery room some decades before, without them ever seeing them. Many years after the event, I have found them to be still grieving over not having had the opportunity to see and hold their baby for a time after their birth, to try to come to terms with what had happened.

Nowadays medical facilities have expanded the physical care of the mother to include her mental and emotional well-being. If you feel that having your baby and all tissues from the pregnancy returned to you would help you and your family through the difficult days to come, this can be arranged. Simply ask the medical staff attending to you to make a note that this is what you want. In most miscarriages, any medical tests performed on your baby to try to establish the cause of their death would be voluntary. If you as the parent chose not to have these tests performed, your baby can be released to go home with you when you are discharged.

LAYING A MISCARRIED BABY TO REST

WHAT YOU CAN CHOOSE TO DO

You can leave your baby at the hospital or medical facility.

If you are comfortable with leaving your baby at the hospital or medical facility for the staff to take care of, you are welcome to do so. Each facility will have their own process of caring for them.

OR

You can take your baby home with you.

If you have chosen to take your baby home with you, here are some ideas for laying them to rest.

CHOOSING CREMATION

Your baby can be cremated at a crematorium. It is important for the parents to realize that when a miscarried baby is cremated, there is usually a very small amount of ash that will be returned to you. Your baby may not need to be brought to the crematorium in a casket. Some crematoriums will accept your baby in a closed box which the family can make or purchase, and decorate themselves. Your baby must just not be visible to the crematorium staff. Some crematoriums may still insist on a formal casket being used. Your funeral director will check with the crematorium regarding this. They will also book the time that you are to arrive, and take care of all necessary paperwork. You can decide how much additional support you will need from your funeral director throughout the funeral process. You as the family are able to take over as much of the funeral as you feel comfortable with.

CHOOSING BURIAL

WHAT YOU CAN CHOOSE TO DO

Your baby can be buried (interred) at home.

Keep in mind that you may want to move at some stage. How would you feel about leaving your baby's burial site? You may want to take them with you. I met a lady who had interred her miscarried baby in a large pot plant. She had a beautiful plant growing in the pot and took comfort in keeping her baby's resting place near to her. She said that if she ever needed to move, she could simply take her pot plant with her. What I took from our conversation is that there are many personal and unique ways to lay your miscarried baby to rest. There are no legal requirements as to how you do this. Allow yourself to think about what you need and what you would be comfortable with over the long term.

OR

Your baby can be interred at a cemetery.

There are special areas at cemeteries just for babies.

OR

You may want to purchase an adult plot and have your baby interred there under the berm.

The berm is the concrete strip at the head of a grave which is the foundation upon which a headstone or plaque is laid. This way both mum and dad can know that one day when they too are interred, they will be together with their baby. Your funeral director will check with the cemetery as to what type of container your baby can be interred in. Some cemeteries will accept your baby for burial in a closed box which the family can purchase or make and decorate themselves, as long as your baby is not visible to the cemetery staff. But some cemeteries may insist on a formal casket being used. Your funeral director will help you to arrange a plot and take care of the necessary paperwork that the cemetery will require.

NOTES

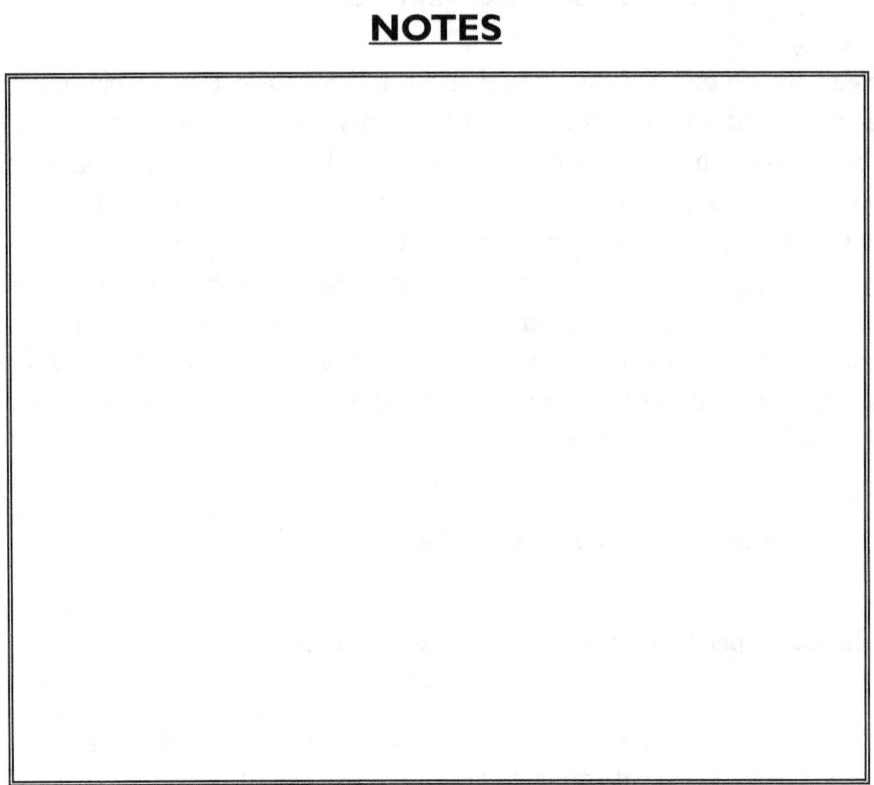

BABIES THAT DIE AND HAVE TO BE REGISTERED WITH THE REGISTRAR OF 'BIRTHS, DEATHS AND MARRIAGES' (BDM) ARE THOSE THAT:

1. Are live-born, regardless of the duration of the pregnancy. Life is confirmed by signs of breathing, a visible heart beat, the pulsation of the umbilical cord or the movement of voluntary muscles.

2. Weigh more than 400g.

3. Have passed 20 weeks in the pregnancy.

4. Have died during the first 28 days of life after their birth.

5. Are older than 28 days from birth.

A legal requirement for all babies who have to be registered with the Registrar of 'Births, Deaths and Marriages', is that they must be buried or cremated at a legal cemetery or crematorium. Your funeral director will help you with all of the paperwork that these facilities will require. They will also make sure that your baby's death is registered.

WHEN A BABY DIES AT A HOSPITAL

Your baby's doctor will need to complete the "cause of death" certificate on your baby's behalf, before they will release them to you.

WHAT YOU CAN CHOOSE TO DO

Once your baby's paperwork is ready, you can leave the hospital with your baby and take them home for a while first, or take them to your funeral home yourself.

OR

You can contact your funeral home from the hospital, and a funeral director will come to help you, and transfer your baby from the hospital to the funeral home mortuary as soon as their paperwork is ready.

When they arrive, they will have a carry cot with them. If you would like your baby's own carry cot to be used, then have it with you and give it to them. Your baby will be wrapped in a blanket and placed inside the carry cot. Your funeral director will take your baby straight to the funeral home mortuary.

You are welcome to follow in your car, and if a family member wants to drive with the funeral director, and hold the baby on the way, they are welcome to do so. On arrival, your baby will be taken into the mortuary, where their body will be cared for.

WHAT YOU CAN CHOOSE TO DO

You can have your baby embalmed.

This makes it possible for you to have more time before their funeral service. This will take some time, as the embalmers give each person they work on the unique treatments and procedures that may be required.

OR

You can choose not to have your baby embalmed.

This can mean that the condition of their body will determine the date for the funeral service, depending on whether you want to take them home, visit with them at the funeral home in the days before the service, or have an open casket on the day of the funeral.

NOTES

DRESSING YOUR BABY

Once your baby's body has been cared for according to your wishes, it is time for them to be dressed.

WHAT YOU CAN CHOOSE TO DO

You can dress your baby yourself.

Your funeral director will help you with this process if you wish. Bring as many outfits as you like to choose from.

OR

You can have your funeral director dress your baby for you.

If you would be more comfortable with this, now is the time to give them the clothes that you have chosen. When your baby is dressed, your funeral director will take you to them in a private room. It is normally fine to pick your baby up and hold them. Stay as long as you need to.

In your baby's casket, favourite blankets can be wrapped around them or used as an extra mattress, and special toys can be placed with them.

NOTES

ONCE YOUR BABY IS DRESSED

WHAT YOU CAN CHOOSE TO DO

You can take your baby home with you, where they will remain until their funeral service.

You can use your own vehicle, or you can ask your funeral director to drive your baby home. You may want to hold them on the way. They can go home to a cot, waiting arms or a bed, and be placed in their casket much later.

OR

You can have your baby remain at the funeral home.

You can spend as much time as you need with them, before leaving them in the care of your funeral director. You can continue to visit them in the days leading up to their funeral service.

NOTES

WHEN A BABY DIES AT HOME UNDER A DOCTOR'S CARE

If a baby dies at home and a family doctor has been caring for the pregnant mother or the born baby, the first thing to do is to phone your family doctor. They may know what the cause of death was and be confident to complete their "cause of death" certificate. If this is the case, an autopsy will usually not be necessary, unless you insist upon it being performed.

The doctor will arrive at your home to confirm that your baby has died. Now is the time to make contact with your funeral home if you have one.

WHAT YOU CAN CHOOSE TO DO

You can have your funeral director come and transfer your baby to their funeral home mortuary as soon as possible.

OR

You can choose a time when you would like your baby to be transferred to the funeral home mortuary, allowing you to spend some time being with them in the privacy of your own home.

When a doctor has been involved with your baby, and they feel that there is no need for an autopsy to be performed, there is generally no urgent need to have them transferred to your funeral home right away. This can possibly be overnight.

If you want to keep your baby home for a time after they have died, I would like to give you some guidelines for their safe keeping:

WHAT YOU NEED TO DO

- Inform your funeral home of your decision to have your baby stay home for a while, and discuss with them a time when they can come.

- Keep your baby cool. If they have been lying on an electric blanket, this needs to be turned off now. If they have been covered by many blankets, remove all but one. If it is winter, do not put a heater on in the room. Allow the room temperature to cool their body. Keep them in the shade. Draw the curtains in summer or winter to protect them from direct sun light. The bacteria designed to break a body down thrive best in warm temperatures.

- In summer, place a fly net or sheet over them if you leave them alone.

If there are signs of rigor mortis, which is stiffening of the joints, do not be concerned. This is a completely natural process and happens in varying degrees to everyone who dies. It is usually very mild in babies.

There are some conditions that may develop concerning your baby's body, when it may be best for them to be transferred to the funeral home mortuary as soon as possible, where they can be kept in a cool room, or embalmed.

- Any areas of blistering or breaks in the skin.
- A strong smell of decomposition.
- Any colour changes on their body.
- Any swelling on their body, especially of the abdomen.

If these conditions are ignored, it may result in their body rapidly breaking down.

If you notice any of these conditions developing, let your funeral director know. If they feel that there is reason for concern, they will come to fetch your baby.

When the funeral director arrives at your home, they will ask for permission to see your baby. They will check what is needed to transfer your baby to their vehicle in a safe and dignified way. When they have told you that they are ready to transfer your baby:

WHAT YOU CAN CHOOSE TO DO

You can stay outside of the room while your baby is placed inside a carry cot.

OR

You can stay in the room to watch the process.

OR

You can help.

If you choose to stay in the room to watch or to help, I will describe what generally happens so that you know what to expect.

- Tell your funeral director that you are ready for them to take your baby.

- They will bring a carry cot into the room. If you want to hug, touch or kiss your baby before they are moved, now is the time to do so.

- They will be placed in the carry cot, and then be safely secured.

- Your funeral director will transfer your baby to their vehicle. You are welcome to assist in carrying them, or to walk alongside. From here they will go directly to the funeral home mortuary.

I have had some families drive behind me to the funeral home where they have remained in a private waiting area until their baby's body has been embalmed. Then we dress them together and take them back home. This may take some hours, but their baby has not been far from those who love them from the time that they died right up to the time when they were brought back to their home, where they remain until the day of their funeral.

NOTES

WHEN THE CORONER IS INVOLVED WITH YOUR BABY

When a baby dies unexpectedly, suspiciously, as the result of an accident, or as the result of a suspected criminal act, and in cases where a doctor has not been involved in the specific treatment of an illness regarding the pregnant mother or her born baby, the coroner will want to perform some form of an autopsy. This is to find out what the cause of the baby's death was.

This can be very hard for the parents and close family to bear because:

1. The parents will be separated from their baby for at least a day while the coroner performs their investigation into the cause of death.

2. The coroner's investigation of a baby is often similar to that performed on an adult, and some of the autopsy incisions may be the same. For the parents who are used to loving and protecting their baby, this can be difficult to see *(refer to the diagram in chapter 3 "what happens to someone when they have an autopsy")*.

NOTES

WHAT TO EXPECT WHEN THE CORONER RELEASES YOUR BABY

It is important that the coroner knows which funeral home you have chosen. As soon as they are finished with their investigation they will contact you and your funeral home.

WHAT YOU CAN CHOOSE TO DO

You can meet your funeral director at the coroner's mortuary, where the coroner will give your baby to them.

They will be wrapped in a blanket and placed into a carry cot. If you would like to give your funeral director your baby's own carry cot to use, you are welcome to do so. Your funeral director will take your baby directly to their mortuary. You are welcome to follow them in your vehicle, and if a family member wants to hold the baby and drive with the funeral director, they are welcome to do so.

OR

You can have your funeral director transfer your baby from the coroners mortuary to the funeral home

mortuary, where you will meet later at an agreed-upon time.

On arriving at the funeral home mortuary, your baby's body will be cared for.

WHAT YOU CAN CHOOSE TO DO

You can have your baby embalmed.

Even though this means even more time away from them, it makes it possible for you to have more time before their funeral service. Also, the sooner they are embalmed, the sooner they can be held without concern. Your baby's body preparations may take some time. It is important to realize that to embalm a baby that has been autopsied can take as long as an autopsied adult might, and sometimes longer.

OR

You can choose not to have your baby embalmed.

This can mean that the condition of their body will determine the date for the funeral service, depending on whether you wanted to take them home, visit with them at the funeral home in the days before the service, or have an open casket on the day of the funeral.

NOTES

DRESSING YOUR BABY

Once your baby's body has been cared for according to your wishes, it is time for them to be dressed.

WHAT YOU CAN CHOOSE TO DO

You can have your funeral director dress your baby.

Have your baby's clothes chosen and ready to give to them. Once your baby is dressed, your funeral director will take you to them in a private room. You should be able to pick them up and hold them. Stay as long as you need to.

OR

You can dress your baby yourself.

If you have decided to be involved in their dressing:
Allow yourself time when you first see them. You may have been separated from your baby for days and this can be an intense and emotional reunion. There is no rush, so do not feel that you have to start dressing straight away. Once you feel ready to begin, lay out all of the clothes that you have brought. It is fine to bring different outfits to see which one will look the best. Your funeral director will help you with the dressing if you wish.
Often babies don't have enough hair to hide the head incision that may have been made in the autopsy. All of the incisions will be neatly sutured by the embalmer, but a hat, cap, hoodie or beanie will hide this completely, and can look like part of a deliberately chosen outfit.
A favourite blanket can be placed in the casket to use as an additional mattress, or even to wrap your baby in once they are dressed. For this reason your funeral director will often prepare a casket for your baby that is quite a bit bigger than you might think would be necessary. This allows room for lots of layers of clothes and blankets. It also provides space for any toys that

you may want to put in with them. This bigger casket will make your baby look comfortable and not cramped, even with a lot of things in the casket with them.

NOTES

TAKING YOUR BABY HOME

If you have decided that you want your baby at home with you for the days before their funeral, here are some guidelines on how to care for them:

You should be able to hold your baby. Your funeral director would have told you if there were any concerns about the condition of your baby that may mean you should leave them in their casket.

Once your baby is home, if they have been touched a lot on their hands and face during the day, a very simple baby moisturiser can be patted onto these areas of contact. This will stop any skin dehydration and possible darkening of these areas. Any excess moisturiser can be lightly patted off with a clean, soft cloth.

In summer, care should be taken to cover your baby with a net or sheet if they are left unattended. It is a good idea to make sure that pets do not have any unsupervised time with your baby. Some well-meaning pets may lick your baby and cause potential damage to often delicate skin.

It is usually once the family have been reunited with their baby that their funeral director will make a time to meet with them. The family can decide what type of funeral they want to have for their baby, or even if they want to have one at all. Their funeral director will help and facilitate them throughout this process.

NOTES

PLACING A NEWSPAPER NOTICE FOR A BABY

The procedure of placing a newspaper notice for a baby is exactly the same as it is for an adult. Some parents derive comfort from placing a notice of their baby's death in the "births" notices as well. The life of their child is acknowledged, and even if their baby did not live long, they did live. You are welcome to do this.

NOTES

LAYING YOUR BABY TO REST

CHOOSING BURIAL

There are infant areas dedicated to little ones in cemeteries. You would have to go to your cemetery of choice to choose a baby plot.

Many parents would like to know that when they die, they will be close to their baby. This is possible if they buy an adult plot and request that their baby be interred under the berm which is the concrete strip at the head side of the grave that a headstone would be placed upon. With a baby casket interred beneath it, the plot is still available for other interments later. The parents can choose to be buried in the same plot when their time comes. This ensures that when mum and dad are interred, they will be together with their baby. This can be a comfort to many of the family and friends at the burial.

If your baby's casket is too big for this area, they may need to be interred in the plot as a standard burial, at a double burial depth. At the time one of the parents die, they can be interred in the same plot as their baby at a single burial depth.

Your funeral director will check with the cemetery what their requirements are regarding the type of container your baby may be interred in. Some cemeteries will accept your baby for burial in a closed box, which the family can make or purchase, and decorate themselves, as long as your baby is not visible to the cemetery staff. Some cemeteries however, may insist upon a formal casket being used.

CHOOSING CREMATION

Your funeral director will check with the crematorium what their requirements are regarding the type of container your baby may be cremated in. Some crematoriums will accept your baby for cremation in a closed box which the family can make or purchase, and decorate themselves, as long as your baby is not visible to the crematorium staff. Some crematoriums however, may insist upon a formal casket being used.

Cremated human remains are known as ashes. They are comprised mostly of calcium from the skeletal bones. Babies have higher water content in their tissue than adults, and less dense bones. They will not have experienced enough stress on their skeleton to store more calcium. These two factors mean that after the cremation process is complete, there will be much less ash than there would be for an adult. If the parents are aware of this, it can prepare them for when they collect their baby's ashes from their funeral director in the days following their baby's funeral. It can also help them to choose a suitably-sized ash urn or other container, should they wish to keep their baby's ashes in something small and personal.

NOTES

CONCLUSION

When a baby dies, we lose the future. Hopes and dreams no longer able to take root, become grief and sadness, that wash their colour over our lives, our relationships. If we are blessed with loving support, good counselling and time, we may still find that this colour will not go away. Perhaps, when it is able to, it will shrink and bend, and take its place as one of the new colours in the rainbow of us. Some experiences have such an impact on us that we are irrevocably changed. Take courage.

REFERENCES

Embalming history, theory and practice by Robert G Mayer (3rd edition)

Information obtained from the New Zealand Ministry of Health

www.ingramcontent.com/pod-product-compliance
Lightning Source LLC
Chambersburg PA
CBHW072203280526
45788CB00002B/861

* 9 7 8 1 4 5 3 8 2 9 7 1 4 *